Keep Going,
Keep Growing

Tim Morris

Table of Contents

"Keep Going, Keep Growing"

My journey from finding love, dealing with loss, finding my purpose and the ability to

Keep Going

Dedication

This book is dedicated to my rockstar wife Tara Morris.

You gave me so much that I must give back.

Your strength and love have helped me to Keep Going.

#TaraForever # TwinFlames

Acknowledgments

I would like to thank "My Why", Tara Nikayja Morris. Without Tara, none of this would be possible. She changed my entire life and there is nothing I can say to thank her. That is why this book is dedicated to her and why I keep going, for her!

I would also like to thank my family; Jerryl and Doris Morris, Melanie Morris and John Vazquez Sr. When the storm is at its worst and it seems like no one else is around, you always have your family. I thank each of you for the part they played in helping me to heal and keep going.

Next, I would like to thank my extended family of brothers. I could not have made it without the love and support from a group of men. I would be disrespecting them if I called them mere friends. Thank you to Jabari Keyton, Cody Elion, Brandon Halton, Sahara Brinson, Julius Thames, Ricky Whitley, Lamonte Cooper, Cyrus Hunter, and Michael Blanchard. There are many more. Please forgive me if I didn't list your name. This group of brothers were there for me from the beginning of this ordeal and still here now. I don't nowhere I would have been if not for these great men.

Through this situation, I not only strengthened my bond with my brothers but gained a group of sisters also. Tara had a huge network of friends that operated as a family. This group of women has become my family. They have added to the support I've received since the Lord chose to take Tara home. Janet Stockdale, Cherrelle King, Rita Givens, Renay McCarty, Antoinette Terragano, Tamara Pugh, Nia Jones, Ashley Wells, Felicia Garza, and Tiana Davis. This group of women has continued to check on me, support me, and pray for me through these tough times. I may have lost my wife, but I gain some more family.

I would like to thank P31 Publishing for providing me with a place that has helped me heal through this process. It was not easy on me emotionally, but I needed to stretch myself to heal. Thank you for everything. I can't leave out my writing consultant Shay McNeil. Out of nowhere she came to my rescue and helped me with the writing process. Huge thank you for all she did.

From the moment Tara was diagnosed, we received support from everywhere. There are so many people whose names I don't even know that supported us in our time of need. Since Tara's passing, I have continued to receive support from many corners of the country and even the world. I can't put into words how grateful I am for that. There is no way I could list every person that has been a part of this healing process. Huge thank you to everyone who ever made a call, sent a text, direct message. I appreciate it and love you! Thank you!

Chapter 1

The Match and Meet

L ife has a funny way of teaching you lessons. I grew up as an athlete. I played baseball and football as a child living in Queens, New York. At 14, my parents moved us from New York City to Atlanta, Georgia. When I got to Georgia, I resumed playing football and baseball. I was on the high school football team and played travel baseball. Throughout high school, when you're an athlete, you typically get special treatment. So, like most athletes, they gave me privileges that many other students were not afforded. One privilege that athletes enjoy is attention from girls. This attention continued into college where you don't have to be an athlete. So, as you can see, high school and college can give you a warped sense of reality when it comes to the opposite sex. Once out of college I walked the streets like I was the biggest ladies' man around. Since I thought I was God's gift to women, I dated frequently and often. Many of these relationships were dead-end relationships; Most of them ended because of something I did or did not do. I never really cared because there were so many women to choose from.

Then one day I met a girl that was different. She was beautiful, educated, and fun to be around. Before I knew it, we were in a relationship. I was about 24 years old at the time. We enjoyed our time together. It was the best relationship I had ever been in. Everything seemed great until my flawed approach to dating kicked in and I lost a great woman. I did everything by the "bad boyfriend playbook". I left myself open to other options (as far as women); I lied, cheated and indulged in activities outside of my relationship that was damaging to her and everything we had built. Even with my bad behavior, I still believed that I loved her but just didn't know how to show that. I didn't know how to not open myself up to other female options. This caused plenty of speculation and loud arguments. One time we even received a visit from the police because of a loud argument in the walkway of our apartment complex. Just like that, I lost a great girl. I found myself back in the dating pool and back to my old habits.

I tried to right my wrongs and treat the next girl like a queen. I turned over a new leaf and thought I was ready to meet a great woman and start a life together. I knew that I had hurt the first girl, so I made sure that didn't happen this time. I did everything different this time around. I stayed away from all temptations. Nightlife became a thing of the past. I used to clean the entire house, cook dinner, mow the lawn and plenty of other things around the house while she was out so it would surprise her when she came home. It felt like we were on track to build a strong extended family. She already had two daughters that I loved taking care of. From the time we met, we saw each other every night and on the weekend. We could only meet at night because she didn't want her girls to see a man coming in and out of the house. The fact that she made such a responsible decision impressed me. I thought to myself, '*There may be something here*'. I hadn't dated a girl that felt that mature before. It may have helped that she was 4 years older than me. This relationship turned out to be my karma relationship. A few months into the relationship, I began noticing some odd behavior from her. She was doing a lot of lying and hiding of minor information. Soon after, I found evidence when I came home early and saw two beer bottles on my side of the bed. She didn't drink beer, so I knew she had someone else in our room on my side of the bed. She told me every lie under the sun. I've always prided myself on being very observant and I knew what I saw and heard was wrong.

The girl I was with was unfaithful. Issues with her child's father and not one but two ex-boyfriends found their way onto my plate. If that wasn't bad enough, she continually used our rent and bill money to buy weed. Because of her mismanagement of our bill money, we started having issues. We were without power, almost evicted, and they repossessed her car. Trying to be a good boyfriend, I went out and got a second job and began spending less money. With her being without a car, I would drop her off at work and then her kids at school. The whole time she was still messing with her children's fathers, both ex-boyfriends and who knows who else. I blinded myself to all of it trying to be the good guy. So as all bad relationships go, it ended, and we went our separate ways. I packed all my stuff and left with no destination. I could drop some big items off in my grandfather's garage. When I was leaving his house, I got a call from a friend named Julius asking me to come by his apartment. I knew that I would be able to stay there for the night and create a plan to get my life back together. When I got there he began telling me about a situation, they were having with their apartment and they were probably going to need to move if they didn't find someone to stay in the spare room. Well, that was perfect for me. I paid him the amount of money he was short of and moved in that night.

Things seemed to level out, and I started living a regular life again. A few years later, I was still living in that area, but I had moved into my own place. I started coaching football. Everything was going well. I was coaching football and baseball and really making an impact. I felt productive again, and I was helping to enrich young athletes. Everything seemed to be falling into place. The only thing missing was a good woman to share it with. A girl I knew from college sent me a message on social media. This seemed perfect. We got reacquainted and soon after started dating. I thought I had finally found *the one*. We had secret crushes on each other in school but never acted on it. Shortly after dating her, some red flags began to surface. We continued on with me believing that there wasn't one perfect person and that everyone has red flags. So, I kept pursuing the relationship. Things kept getting worse and eventually I decided that it would not work. The big issue was that a month earlier she had convinced me to move in with her rather than me getting a new apartment when my lease was up. Against my better judgment, I sold most of my stuff and moved in with her. That was one of the biggest mistakes I've made in my dating career. When it became time for me to end the relationship and leave, she made it more difficult than I believed it should have been. Since the situation had gotten bad enough that I never wanted to come home, I decided to just take the plunge and leave. I called a friend of mine, Sahara. He is a close friend of mine that owned a big house. He had been trying to get me to rent out the bottom level of the house from him for several years. Now was the perfect time to take him up on that offer. I called him and confirmed that the offer still stood. When he said yes, I told him I would be there within the week. And just like that, I packed up what I could take and left. I left my flat-screen TV, a DVD player, a trophy case and a few other personal things. Getting out of there was more important than anything else at that time. I then began living on the bottom floor of Sahara's house. That setup worked out great, and I was at peace again. I may have had nothing but the clothes I left with, but I wasn't in a bad situation anymore. I decided to focus on bettering myself and the situation so that nothing like the past few years would happen again. After a few months of working, hustling and living below my means, I thought it would be a good idea to get out and at least start meeting people. I would go out with Sahara and friends to different clubs and lounges. I was unable to ever make a genuine connection with anyone I met.

To make matters worse I was starting to have car issues. It was like I was cursed. Everything I had always turned bad. Eventually, my car died, and I had to start taking mass transit to work. I even walked to work a few times. That was embarrassing and hard to deal with. So, dating was placed on the back burner.

One day on the radio, I heard a radio show host talking about a dating app. I didn't pay much attention and thought it was a watered-down version of another social media network that just showed pictures for you to like. I played with it for a couple of days but didn't get it so; I deleted it and went back to feeling bad about myself. Two days later, the same radio show had an even more in-depth conversation about this app. So, I tried it again wondering if I missed something. I downloaded the app and created a profile, then started swiping. I could have only been swiping for a couple of minutes when I came across a woman that caught my attention. So, what did I do? I Swiped Right! Little did I know what that one small decision would become. Once she came across my profile, she too swiped right. At that moment we were "matched". One day out of nowhere, I got a message from a woman named Tara T. We then exchanged messages for a couple of days and the conversation was great. The only problem was that I was very slow in responding since I was not much of an online social person and dating had become a very difficult thing for me.

One day on a lunch break, I received an angry message from her stating that if I didn't want to talk to her, then don't waste her time. That wasn't the case, so I explained to her how I was not used to communicating through apps or dating sites. I am still a phone call, text or in-person kind communicator. She sent me her phone number with a message that said: "Ok, we'll see!" So, I immediately texted her, so I didn't look like I was just playing around with her. She then sent me a message that read "So when are you going to take me out?" Since I was in such a bad place, I had not even thought about trying to take her out yet. She put me on the spot and almost tested my manhood, so I asked her to dinner on Friday night. I typically would have found a way to be busy. This time I didn't do that. There was something about her that made me not flake. We *matched* and now had a meeting set up.

On the following Friday, I rented a car. We made plans to meet at a lounge downtown called Cloud IX. I chose a lounge, so if she was crazy or a catfish, I could easily exit with no issues. It also gave me room to adjust the rest of the date by how the first part went. If she was cool, I had one plan. If she wasn't or less attractive than her pictures, I had another plan. She beat me to the lounge and was standing at the bar when I walked in. Something about the dress and shoes she had on caught my attention the moment I walked in the door. I didn't know it was her because her back was to me. At that exact moment I looked at her she turned around and look at me. I was very excited to see a face I remembered from the dating app. She was even more beautiful than her pictures, so I was immediately excited and nervous. We greeted each other with a nice hug and found a table. From the moment we sat down it was clear that we had great chemistry and plenty to talk about. The connection was undeniable. We shared some very similar stories. It couldn't have gone any better. After about 20 minutes, I noticed she kept pulling the top of her dress up even though it wasn't sagging or low. She noticed me noticing her, then came right out with it. "I JUST BEAT BREAST CANCER" is what she told me.

She then explained that she had just beat breast cancer but still had to do radiation. She was pulling on her dress because she didn't want me to see her radiation stickers. She proceeded to tell me her entire cancer journey as I sat with my jaw on the floor. I had never heard of someone beating cancer in the way she did. And more than just beating it, it was amazing how she beat it. She was alone with just her little dog. Her boyfriend was in New York and barely even checked on her during the whole ordeal. She drove herself home from chemotherapy, woke up and drove herself to radiation early in the morning multiple times a week and spent all the terrible days at home with only Max her dog to keep her company. She told me a story about the day she had a terrible chemo treatment and was feeling so bad it took her a couple of hours to get home. Once she got home, all she could do was lay in the bed. While lying in the bed, she began to feel and believe she was about to die. She explained to me that in those moments she believed she was going to die in her bed by herself. This next part broke my heart. She described becoming resigned to the fact she was going die, grabbed Max and held him until her eyes closed and she drifted off. Thankfully for everyone, she did not pass away. She woke up a day later with little Max still lying next to her. He didn't even use the bathroom during that time. Max was a good dog; he would never leave her side.

After she told me the story, she told me it was ok if that was TOO much, and if I wanted to end the date, she wouldn't have any hard feelings. That statement appalled me somewhat since I know how hard fighting cancer can be. I told her I was in awe of her and her strength. I told her she was far stronger than I ever thought I could be. She became my hero at that moment and I think that's when I fell in love. I then began to tell her how my dad and mom had cancer-related issues in the past that they both worked through and are fine. I was able to make her understand that not only do I understand but that would not be a reason for me to not date her. So, since the date was going so great, after dinner we went to a party my friends were throwing and continued to have an amazing time. It was great; I didn't have to use my backup plan. From that night forward, there was no person I wanted to spend more time with than Tara Turnbough. We were completely inseparable from that night on.

Chapter 2

The Relationship

Tara was a very different person from anyone I had ever met, let alone dated. She was so different from what I was used to; I was immediately taken with her. We were two completely opposite people. She had a super type A personality. There were times she could be very mean and dominating. At any moment she could snap and there was no stopping her. I wasn't sure I would be able to handle this woman. She was far wilder than any person I had met. She was very smart and controlled at the same time. She had a past that made me question if she could be someone for me. She was used to being around and dating people that made a lot more money than me and was not shy about talking about it. She was exactly the girl I would never have entertained in the past. Just as she was completely opposite of anything I was used to or wanted, I wasn't really her type of guy either. While I was wondering about her, she was having the exact same thoughts. I was so torn between continuing to talk to this woman that I would try to avoid her from time to time but I just couldn't. I had a connection and attraction to her that was far stronger than I had ever felt before. Fearing I might make a bad decision

I sought the counsel of one of my closest friends Cody. Cody and I are close like brothers. I would call him my brother to people. After a deep conversation with Cody, I was reminded that everyone has a past and if it's not showing up in the current situation, then why let something potentially great pass by. That was the best advice I have ever received.

Tara and I began dating seriously immediately. We decided that we were going to build a real relationship that could stand the test of time. We spent no more than 10 total nights apart for the entirety of our relationship. Since she didn't have a conventional job she wasn't beholden to a work schedule. She would come stay with me at my place during the week and dropped me off at work. Then on the weekend, I would go to stay at her place. This worked out great. We even began to pray together every morning before I went into work. It was a completely different relationship than any other I had been in. It was the same for her too.

Things got very serious quickly. Even though it was a struggle and a process to blend two different lives, we both leaned on a promise we made to each other on night one. We promised that if we wanted to be with each other we would be completely honest good or bad and always make sure the other felt love all the time. So, proving that she had no secrets, she told me her entire life story. She wanted me to know how she got to where she was at that moment. Her story was a *New York Times* Best Seller.

Her story starts with a broken home that had two parents with their own sets of issues to deal with. Both dealt with those issues in their own ways. Unfortunately, she didn't figure into those plans. She was a young girl with little to no guidance. Her father moved to Texas and would drop in from time to time but was not there as much as she needed. That relationship was on and off for years. Around the age of eight, her mom contracted an aggressive form of cancer. She spent the next four years caring for her mother rather than being a child. She had to take care of her mother and eventually watch her die as a young girl. This led to her being bounced around from family member to family member's house and friend to friend's house. Her father eventually paid for an apartment for her to live in as a teenager. He also bought her a car and then went back to his life. She then began to live an adult's life as a young teenager. She had no choice but to figure it out. When she graduated high school, she went to college in Texas but quickly figured out it wasn't for her. She left college and joined the Air Force where she served her country proudly while traveling the world.

The Air Force, unfortunately, followed in the same path as many of her past life experiences. It turned bad. During her time in the service, she witnessed and received terrible treatment by the powerful male superiors. She was even a witness to a suicide caused amid a domestic dispute between friends. These experiences helped cause some mental issues such as PTSD and the Manic-Depressive trait. How could it not? She was eventually medically discharged and moved to Phoenix with a cousin. This cousin worked at an adult strip club and convinced her to try it. She needed to make some money, and it seemed like easy work. She tried it and was lukewarm to it. The living situation wasn't the greatest, so she relocated to Houston.

Now in Texas, she picked up where she left off and jumped back into the club. In Texas, strippers didn't take their clothes off, so she found an avenue to exploit that while making some money. She could use her God-given talents. What talent is that? The gift of gab and the ability to connect with ANYONE. She created a legion of followers by being a genuinely interesting and charismatic person. This helped her build a strong client base. She then expanded to party promoting, hosting, and started a blog.

She gained quite a name for herself through blogging. She made many friends and even more enemies. She engaged in online battles with multiple celebrities and somehow always came out the other side clean. She was successful in every move she made. Successful at everything except dating. She spent the next few years dating all the wrong men and even some women. She was open to anything that may bring her happiness. A very bad relationship forced her to move to Dallas abruptly. When she moved to Dallas, her entrepreneurial passions were at an all-time high. She knew how to get what she wanted when she wanted it. She even figured out she didn't have to sleep with men to get what she wanted. That was the successful approach that she even taught other girls.

In the relationship realm, she still could not find success. Abusive relationship after abusive relationship she continued searching. She eventually moved to Atlanta to start over. With only her car, some trash bags and a few thousand dollars, she began her next life adventure. She had a boyfriend, but he lived in New York. She rarely saw him. She knew he was cheating, but he paid the bills and was 800 miles away so what could she do? She stayed and just continued reaping the financial benefits while not receiving anything else to help build her up. Everything was fine until her world was rocked in November 2013. After an odd situation in which her dog Max began scratching at her left breast, she noticed it seemed bigger than the other breast. A couple of days later she went to the doctor to check it out. What she found out would change her life and the life of a man she hadn't even met yet. Life was throwing her a curveball she never could have imagined. Tara was diagnosed with stage 4 breast cancer and lymphoma. This was a huge punch in the stomach. Stage 4 Cancer means that cancer has spread to other parts of the body, therefore, making it much more difficult to fight and defeat. She was devastated, but the fighter that had seen everything in life didn't stay down long. She immediately started aggressive treatment. She had to go through and endure this treatment completely alone.

After conferring with her doctor and taking her family history into account, she decided to have a double mastectomy, chemotherapy, and radiation. This was a life-changing event. For a woman whose looks were an enormous part of her, this was a huge decision. She was in for the fight of her life and her boyfriend didn't assist other than sending money. Through all of this, she had her surgery, attended her treatments and against all odds, won. She beat it. She was cancer-free. Other than some follow up radiation treatments, she was done. Fast forward to August 29, 2014, Tara took a chance on a completely different man than she would have ever dated. She figured if she wanted different results she had to do something different. So, she gave me a shot.

Things weren't exactly easy in the beginning. Tara and I came from completely different places. We didn't have the same views of the world. Had we met in a different way at a different time, there would have been no chance we would have ever got together. She was just stepping away from the party girl life but still had a lot of it in her. On the other hand, I left that world years ago and social life was the last thing on my mind. I was in the middle of dealing with an issue with my car. The issue was that I had no car. It had gone down with mechanical issues that were very expensive. During this time of year, I was coaching football. I would take a taxi or even walk to work in the morning and in the afternoon, I would take a taxi, bus, and train to football practice. Since it was football season, I was very busy during the week. Once Tara and I started seeing each other, I would rent cars on the weekend to go see her or to go out. That differed greatly from the life she was used to living.

She was traveling all around the country having a good time. She wasn't tied to anything and had financial freedom.

I went to work every day and was just barely getting by. She didn't have a regular job and was completely free. She looked at me like I was less than a man in the beginning. I couldn't tell you why she continued to talk to me because at that time she looked at me like a peasant. I guess it was my glowing personality that won her over. Yeah, right! She used to tell me that she saw something in me and believed I could be great. That said, a lot about her. That was not how she operated in the past. We, of course, had some growing pains in the early stages of our relationship. It was going to be a relationship that had to be constantly worked on. It wasn't easy, but we had a goal of building a strong, long-lasting relationship. Through that, we still fell in love quickly and started making plans for our future. I started taking off on days that she had doctor's appointments so that I could go with her as she finished her treatment. I knew this woman was going to need the support she had never received. She may have beat up cancer without any help, but I knew that she would still need someone to support her. Even after being told she was cancer-free, she still had to deal with the effects of all the treatment. She had a double mastectomy, lost most of her hair and a lot of weight. I would lay in bed many nights praying for the strength to be the best man possible for this amazing woman. I didn't want to confide in anyone about it yet. I felt like everyone would tell me not to involve myself in a relationship that started out with issues. Fortunately, I am not the kind of person to bail on anyone even if we are just in the beginning stages. I knew we would be in for a stressful experience but all I could see was the great ending to this story. Nobody could tell me we were not going to create a life together that would be an example of what strength and love can do if you focus your energies in the right place. We were building an unbreakable relationship.

Chapter 3

The Trip

Like most relationships, we started out having an amazing time. We were still having an amazing time even after that 90-day period that most relationships where things start to change. This was amazing because I know in the past I have been the one who changed after the initial honeymoon period. In our case, every day felt like the honeymoon period. Ironically, just after that 90-day period, we planned a trip together. It was like an actual honeymoon. In December of that year, we decided to take our first trip together. We traveled to Colorado to hang with her family around the holidays with the main goal for me to meet her dad. Her dad wasn't the friendliest person at that time. We had never spoken on the phone and when she spoke about me, he never seemed to care. This trip would prove to be a huge moment in our relationship. I met her father, stepmother, her sister, and her two childhood friends. It was a great time with family. We did everything from going to a comedy show, to lunch with 20 plus members of her family and even went to the zoo. There was no way we were going to go to Colorado and not stop by a dispensary. We picked up some goodies and went to a nice rooftop party and had fun like we always would. We didn't have a care in the world at that time. We simply enjoyed each other's company. Having the opportunity to meet her family and friend was an honor. She never brought her boyfriends around her family. Even more impactful was that she wanted me to meet her father who had met none of her boyfriends. He never really cared to meet them. To be honest I was nervous meeting a parent for the first time in my life. My nervousness didn't come from worrying about how he felt about me. I was nervous about how Tara would feel after his response. Even though they had a strained relationship she was still a daddy's girl and it was extremely important to her for him to accept me even if he didn't care to have a relationship with me. We met her dad and his wife for lunch the day we arrived, but went and spent a few hours with him a couple of days later. Everything seemed ok. Her dad was not a man who showed much emotion or ever give any validation. I just hoped it was a good enough meeting to keep her at ease.

On our last day in Denver, we went to visit her mother's grave. Just as we were pulling into the cemetery a song began playing on the radio called *"Sure Gonna Miss Her"*. I heard it, but I was concentrating on finding where we were going. Out of the corner of my eye, I noticed Tara was crying. I asked what happen and she asked if I was listening to the song. I hadn't been listening, but the song completely applied to the feelings she was having at that moment. The song was about missing a family member that was very near and dear to the singer's heart, but he never got a chance to tell her everything he really felt. These are the exact same thoughts and feelings I knew Tara had in the loss of her mom all of those years ago. All the emotion came rushing back at that moment. The mood in the car became very heavy. We made it to the gravesite and sat in the car for a few moments in silence. I didn't want to speak and interrupt the moment. After a few minutes, we got out of the car and walked to the grave. As we stood there reflecting and praying something interesting happened as I held her. Out of nowhere, it began snowing. There was no snow in the forecast and we didn't even have coats on. At that moment she turned to me with tears streaming down her face and said this was the most perfect moment in her life. This moment could only be given by God. She hugged me as tight as she could and told me that this is exactly where we were supposed to be at that exact moment. From the song on the radio to the snow, to this extremely intense feeling of our soul fusing into one. It was a deeper feeling than I had ever had before. While holding her at that moment, I felt more connected to her than I had to anyone else in life. The moment almost took on a spiritual feeling. After a while, we left to head to the airport to return home. That day the term Twin Flame was discovered. I had always grown up hearing about soul mates. I believed that was the perfect match for a person. It was our belief that you can have more than one soul mate. Twin Flames, on the other hand, are perfect mirrors to each other. That is far more uncommon than a soul mate. We believed that we are Twin Flames and God put us on earth to find each other. We found each other, and an unparalleled love was created. The ride to the airport was the most peaceful ride we have ever taken. In a final extraordinary incident, we missed the exit we needed to get to the airport which forced us to take another route. The route we took ended up being the most beautiful ride we ever took together. We had the most beautiful, peaceful view of the Rocky Mountains as we traveled to the airport. We rode in perfect silence as we headed home from a truly amazing trip.

Chapter 4

The Return

We made it back to Atlanta with more hope for the future than we ever had before. The trip was confirmation that we belonged together. That feeling didn't last very long. Upon our return to Atlanta, she began experiencing intense pain all over her body but mostly concentrated in her back. We went to the doctor to see what was wrong. After running a few tests, the doctor came in the room told us that all her tests came back normal. We were happy but confused as to where this pain could be coming from. The doctor left for a few minutes and then came back and informed us that they had found some spots on her liver and her spine. They said it could be nothing or it could be something they have to investigate. I became instantly confused and a little scared. I wasn't sure what I feared, but something felt wrong. We both became freaked out even though I played strong for her. A few days went by, and I received a call at work. The call was to my cell phone, but I couldn't answer. Then a few moments later my work phone rings with her number on the caller ID. I knew it couldn't be good news. I answered the call and all I could hear was hysterical crying and screaming. My heart broke into a million pieces at that moment. I knew what it was already. I told her I would go outside and call her from my cell phone. The walk from my desk to the parking lot felt like it was a mile. I can compare it to one of those Spike Lee movies where the main character is standing still and everything else moves around them. I fearfully called her back. When I got her on the phone she was screaming "It's everywhere. It's spread everywhere!". She was referencing that her cancer had come back and spread to numerous areas of her body. My world shook listening to those words through the phone. We both cried together until she told me I can't cry. She said that one of us had to be strong and she didn't have it in her. So, I calmed down and started to try and support and build her up. She told me that the doctor informed her that cancer had returned and had spread to her bones. She was diagnosed with Metastatic Bone Cancer. She was devastated. I was also but I was not able to show it. I had to become an actor. She needed me to be the man she needed. I wasn't ready but there was no time to worry about that. She even stated that she finally found a man that loves her for her, we had started talking about marriage, and she had even started thinking about having more than one baby. I was distraught also. I couldn't figure out how someone so strong, so loving, so amazing just couldn't get a break. I knew then my life was now in a different place. We made a pact to beat this as a team and lead a regular life. I wasn't going anywhere, and I wasn't going to let her ever feel alone. Part of continuing our regular life was to continue to do the things that made us happy. So that is what we did.

In early January we were blessed to win a vacation. We were given a choice of locations and we chose New Orleans. She loved New Orleans and I had never been there before. So, we planned the trip. We were back to doing what we love to do. Traveling was always a great way for us to get away from the hard days. It was great to do something like this together with everything we had gone through.

When we got to New Orleans we did the normal "New Orleans things". We walked Bourbon Street and had some drinks and food. We watched an awesome street performance. I watched her smile like she was having the time of her life during the show. I was at peace at that moment because I knew she wasn't thinking about any illness or pain at that moment. After a while, we decide to go back to the hotel and get some rest before we found a party to go to later that night. That is when the trip took a turn for the worst. When we got back to the room she started experiencing severe pain. We decided to take a nap and hopefully, she would feel better when we woke up. While laying down the pain kept intensifying. It got so bad that she couldn't even lay down. All she was able to do was sit straight up and try not to hurt anything. I wasn't able to comfort her. The pain was so bad it hurt for me to touch her. This was extremely difficult for me. I had become accustomed lightly rubbing her back when she was in pain. She reluctantly asked for me not to rub her back because even the light touching was painful. We spent hours just sitting there with me occasionally being able to lightly rub her back. I decided to call it a night and we spent the rest of that night trying to get her comfortable enough to go to sleep. After some hours passed we were able to lay down and finally go to sleep.

The next morning, we woke up, and everything was ok. We chose to start our day with a nice breakfast. After breakfast, we walked around Canal Street and then down by the water. Since she was in a weakened state we had to stop a few times and just sit. Those times gave us a chance to stay engaged with each other. We would joke around, and people watch. She took me to the world-famous Café De Monde. We shared some beignets and enjoy the city. After running some errands, we had to get her some crawfish from her favorite crawfish restaurant. She was not about to be in New Orleans and not enjoy her favorite food, from her favorite seafood spot. Just like the night before we decided to go back to the room and relax for a while. She needed to take breaks throughout the day to rest. We went back to the room and took a nap. During our nap, I was awakened by a loud shout. It was Tara crying out in pain. The pain had come back quickly. We spent the rest of that day and night tending to her pain. The pain was far more intense this time. So much so that I spent that time terrified. We spent the rest of the afternoon, evening, and most of the night trying to make her comfortable. It was one of the longest nights we ever had. We spent most of the time crying and praying for relief of the pain. We were finally able to get her to sleep at around 3:30 am. I was so stressed out and so emotionally weak that I had to leave the room and take a walk around the block. I needed a good cry but was unable to find a spot not populated with people. I finally chose to sit on the steps of someone's house and cry my eyes out for about fifteen minutes. After that fifteen minutes was up I was back in the room. I was unable to be away from her for more than 20-30 minutes. I decided that the next day we would leave earlier than we had planned. I felt that she needed to be home. So, the next morning, I got up early and packed up the car. I put her in the car around 8:30 am and hit the road.

We returned home from New Orleans on Monday, Feb 9th. It was a rough trip due to the intense pain episodes she was having. She fell asleep as soon as we got in the truck. She slept the entire ride home, only waking up once when I stopped to eat. When we finally got home I had to carry her upstairs and put her in the bed that night. She did not leave the bed for a week. It was ok for the first couple of days then I began to get concerned. I may have been concerned but my only job was to make her feel as good as possible so that was what I did. I served her all meals in bed, did all of the household chores and spent as much time as I could trying to lift her spirits. We would even lay in the bed and talk for hours about everything from pop culture and social media to what our future would look like.

We had talked about our future together for a long time. I knew a long time ago that she would be my wife eventually and even got a ring. I planned out a few proposals but wasn't sure when and how I was going to do it. On Feb 14th

Valentine's Day, I planned to take her to a nice restaurant and then go to the big Ferris wheel in the city. We couldn't do any of that because if the condition she was in. I changed the plans and choose to buy her some flowers, balloons and cook her a nice dinner. I planned it as a surprise, so I waited for her to take a nap before I cooked. She woke up while I was gone and called me to check on me. In the little girl voice, she would use to get things out of me she said "Baby I woke up to you not being here and was scared. I wanted to cry but then remembered that you would never leave me". That moment touched my heart. I knew I couldn't live without her and she couldn't live without me. As I pulled into the driveway I decided that there would never be a perfect moment to officially "pop the question". This moment seemed like the perfect time. I grabbed the ring out of the car and marched upstairs so see her smiling face as I walked in. Even though she was in bed I was going to propose to her. She was laying in bed feeling well and happy, so I thought the opportunity was great. I grabbed the ring and the balloons and flowers I bought. I gave her the balloons, flowers, and card first. While she was reading the card, I got down on one knee with the ring out. When she looked up at me and saw the ring she just smiled. She couldn't muster the energy to get excited, but then again, we had already talked about it. Even still, I formally asked her to marry me. She asked me to get up and give her a hug while saying "I was already going to marry you. Now come lay down". I then laid down and we took a nap. When we woke up I served her dinner and we watched the NBA all-star game together.

When it was over she told me, she needed to go to sleep because she was hurting bad and feeling very weak. I asked her how serious she felt it was. She told me she thinks she may need to go to the ER. I told her we should go right now. She said she wasn't strong enough to get up and she needed to rest for a little while. That little while turned into sleeping till about 4:00 am. That was when she couldn't take it anymore. She woke me up and said she needs to go to the emergency room. We got and went to the ER and were eventually checked into the hospital. This trip to the hospital proved to be very different than any of the previous times. We would usually go, and she would get her test done or she would receive fluids and that would be all we needed. After some test were ran we just waited. After about an hour the ER doctor came back and said they would be admitting her to ICU and would come get us when a bed was ready. I didn't understand why we needed to do all that if she was just dehydrated, which was the case the previous time. This was very weird, and I questioned what the issue was and why she had to be admitted. They told me the situation was very serious and they had to treat her right away. I could not understand what they were telling me, so they found another doctor to talk to me. A very nice doctor came and took me in the hallway and explained to me that her calcium levels were extremely high and needed to be treated. The doctor was using terms like life-threatening heart failure, and brain damage. The calcium levels in her body have spiked to life-threatening levels.

We were then admitted to the hospital where she stayed for six weeks. The first few days were very tense. The doctors proceeded to tell me that she was in a life-threatening position for the first 3 days. The doctor told me that we came in just in time. Had we waited longer there is a good chance she could have slipped into a coma and passed away. These were earth-shattering words that were being said to me. This situation flipped the switch in my head. I was not in caregiver mode. I didn't leave the hospital for the first 6 days. I spent the first 2 weeks straight in the hospital only leaving for food and to get clothes. I didn't even go to work. This situation was the scariest thing I had ever gone through.

I could not comprehend what was happening. I was lost but all I could do was comfort my woman as much as possible. Since she told me I had to be strong for both of us, I had to be creative in how I released my own stress. I would wait until she went to sleep, then I would walk to the car and spend an hour crying and praying. Every emotion possible would pass through my head. I would flip back and forth between scared, angry and confused depending on the moment. I was a basket case but had no way to calm or comfort myself.

Many nights I would sit in the car and talk to my great friend Brandon. We have been friends for 14 years. He would stay up on the phone with me and just give the encouragement I would need to make it through the night. The time we spent on the phone would help me get through the night and then I was back to worrying in the morning. If I went to work the next day we would take our lunch break together and he would just sit and listen to me. This was how I would make it through the day. This became a ritual that I absolutely needed in order not to lose it mentally. We could not afford for me to fall apart. With the sense of calm, I would have after our talks, I would return to our room and spend the rest of the night trying to relax in a more positive mood. I don't know what I would have done without that outlet, but Brandon was a lifesaver.

Those positive restful nights were short-lived though. Nurses used to come into our room between 4:00 am and 6:00 am every day to check Tara's vitals. It became very difficult for her to be poked and prodded every day. It seemed like every other day she was being taken downstairs for more testing. This became very stressful for her. When she was stressed out I was stressed out. All we could do was lean on each other. We had gotten pretty good at that.

When doctors are running certain tests, they must ask female patients if they are pregnant. We never once thought about her being pregnant since we were unable to have sex for some weeks due to the pain she was experiencing. On this specific day, the test they needed to run was so dangerous for a pregnant woman that they did not ask if she was pregnant, they just did a pregnancy test first. To our surprise, the test came back positive. This was quite a shock to both of us. We had no clue that she was pregnant. We were so happy and a little bit scared due to her health situation. Since she had been eating very healthy and taking all her vitamins and supplements we believed that everything would be ok. Tara who never wanted children was about to have her first child. As for myself, I've always wanted kids, so this was great. I was going to have a child with the most special person in my life. This was one of the biggest highlights of my life. We were going to create a life together. As connected as we were this was a deeply amazing feeling. The doctor ordered the Obstetrician-Gynecologist (OBGYN) to come visit us. They came the same day and talked to us about pregnancy during this difficult time. They then ordered a sonogram to check out the baby. Later that afternoon three OBGYN doctors came with the sonogram machine. Upon the first look, they stated that the baby was between nine and ten weeks old. That made sense because that would have put the conception date right around when we got back from Denver, and that was the last time we had sex. While they were showing the figure of the baby on the screen I could see the happiness on her face. It was like nothing I had ever seen from her before. She had already converted into mommy mode. She had an amazing glow. After a few minutes, I saw the sonogram technician playing with the views. Then one told the other they were having trouble finding the heart. At that point, Tara didn't know what they were doing. I was able to see the concern on the doctor's face. Then the doctor said the words that I will never forget. "We cannot find the heart," she said; she then showed us where it was supposed to be. Everything else looked good except for the dark spot where the heart should be glowing in the machine. They spent about 15 minutes trying to find the beating heart. They even went as far as to reconfigure the machine. At last, with great regret, they told us that the baby had been lost. It was their belief that the baby had died very recently. Our entire world came crashing down at that moment.

We went from as happy as we could possibly be to completely broken and defeated again. There was no way for me to console her, let alone process it myself. All I could do was ask "God *why?*" We spent the next few hours crying together and wondering why it was that we must go through all of this. It appeared we were cursed and nothing good would ever happen for us. We had made friends with an amazing ICU nurse named Martene. She had helped us since the day we were admitted to the hospital. She came in after the doctors left. She had visibly been crying herself. She stayed with us and consoled us while we cried. She then said that she would come back when she got off work. When she got off she came back and prayed with us. She asked if it would be ok for her to bring her mom up to the hospital to pray with us. We were ok with that. Within a day or two, her mom was at the hospital praying over Tara and our family. We didn't know a stranger could care so much. We then began the process of trying to heal and keep going. Since Tara was in a bad physical condition we knew that we had to refocus on getting Tara back healthy but that was going to be difficult since everything seemed to be going wrong.

My birthday was that Saturday, but I wasn't concerned about it at all. My only concern was Tara and her health. One the other hand, my birthday was very much a concern for her. Secretly, she had asked a few of her friends to pick me up a cake and a bunch of balloons. On Saturday we received a knock at the door and in came three very beautiful girls with a cake and about 30 balloons of varying sizes, shapes and styles. A few minutes later a few more came to the room. Tara had planned a mini birthday party in our hospital room from her bed. She was such an amazing person. Even in her darkest hour she still was able to think about me and do her best to make my birthday a good experience. She said she felt bad I had to spend my birthday in the hospital. I didn't mind being there with her one bit. This gesture touched me deeply. The level of her selflessness was amazing. Of all my birthdays, that birthday will never be forgotten. With that gesture, Tara showed me that even in a bad situation she was able to keep going. I already loved her with all my heart, but that made my love for her even stronger. There is nothing I wouldn't do for this woman.

As the days went by I would go home from time to time to feed the dog, get more clothes for work, and pick up things she wanted. Knowing she would be getting better and would be going home soon, I went home on Saturday morning and decorated the house so that whenever she was discharged she would come home to a nice welcome home gesture.

As the weeks went on, she began to gain strength and was released 6 weeks after she was admitted. We were finally going home. When we walked into the house she really loved the "Welcome Home" signs, balloons and flowers. Her favorite dinner was already cooked and ready to eat. She had returned home, and she had returned to the woman she was before this situation. She came home and was better than she had been in a long time. She was even able to get back to working out a few times a week. We enjoyed getting back to normal life. We understood how close to death she was. She might not have known but I was fully aware and made a vow I would spend my life making hers easier.

We also went back to traveling. In May I had a baseball tournament in Orange Beach that was a week long. She had some medical appointments that week and was not going to be able to come until later that week. That was going to be too much time apart for us, so she rescheduled the appointments and showed up in Orange Beach a day and a half after me and surprised me. I couldn't have been happier. My beautiful queen had surprised me on this beautiful beach that I couldn't wait to share with her. We had a great time that week and made more memories together. That trip increased our desire to have a destination wedding. We got to work as soon as we got home.

The next several months were spent planning our destination wedding. By September we couldn't wait any longer, so we chose to get married on our own. On September 6, 2015, at 12:00 pm in Laurel Park in Marietta, we were officially married by a close friend of ours Kendall Ficklin. It was an amazing feeling to make such a huge step in our lives. We would be joined forever.

In November, we decided to travel to Cape San Blas, Florida to attend my family's annual Thanksgiving trip to the beach. By this time Tara had lost some weight and wasn't quite as strong as she had been for the past few months. Because of her weakened state, we spent most of the 5 days in bed. The best time we had was cooking Thanksgiving dinner together, I made the turkey and cornbread and she made everything else. We made a large dinner for my family. This was a big change from the Thanksgiving dinners my family had been used to, but that was Tara. She did everything big.

Even though we couldn't do very much, it was still a good trip. It didn't matter if we were home hanging out or traveling the world. We just loved being in each other's company. It didn't matter where.

That year for Christmas, we did not travel to Denver like we usually did. I was unable to make it so Tara scheduled to go for a few days by herself. Tara went for three days to see her dad and put flowers on her mom's grave as she did every year. I had to drop her off at the airport. Dropping her off at the airport that weekend was one of the hardest moments we had together. Having to watch someone else push her in a wheelchair was heartbreaking; that was my job. It killed me not having her near me. Knowing that she was weak and in pain made it emotionally harder to deal with.

I arrived at the airport early, parked, and waited in a close waiting area. Seeing her come off the elevator in that wheelchair with a smile on her face almost made me cry. She was so happy, energetic and without pain. Whenever she was able

to be around family and loved ones she would always be reju-
venated. She would experience no pain or weakness when she
was around family. It was like the love of family was the best
medicine. It's funny how love can make you feel so much better.
I was elated to have her home.

Chapter 5

The Wedding

Upon her return from Colorado, we continued planning our wedding. We had chosen Puerto Rico, but those plans changed to ensure that her father could attend. He was unable to fly so we chose Las Vegas for the location. We did all the planning and financing ourselves. We made sure she had everything she wanted for our special day. Since we had been through so many difficulties, making our wedding the most enjoyable event possible was the ultimate goal.

January turned into a very difficult month. We had a short hospital stay because her resting heart rate was around 135 BPM daily. That was extremely terrifying to me because I was always scared that something could happen with her heart. Throughout the entirety of our relationship, we vowed to pray together daily. The praying increased. We were praying multiple times a day. It was a very emotional time; the only thing we had to lean on was our faith. We were planning a wedding and the stress of her increasing health issues was beginning to weigh on us both. I knew I needed to find a way to relieve my stress an emotion. I could not find anything to do. My personal issues seemed to pale in comparison to the war she was having with her body. It may have been damaging to me, but I was willing to give all of myself to her.

Her condition worsened to the point that a few people asked for us to postpone the wedding. Reluctantly, I went and talked with her about it; however, there was no way the wedding was going to be postponed. She was a very headstrong person. There was no one on earth who could change her mind when it was made up. Not only were their requests ignored, but she directed me to press on even harder, and to tell anyone who didn't agree that they could stay home. This woman was a fighter and would never be deterred from anything. If it was just the two of us we would be ok with that. There was no possible way I was going to tell her no on anything pertaining to this wedding. Instead, I created a healthy meal plan and a mild exercise program for her to build up as much strength as possible. She may not have been able to walk far or for long, but we walked laps in the house a couple of times a day. The new diet and exercise regimen worked well enough. By the week of the wedding, she was able to walk better and stand longer. She had built up more strength than she had in months. In case she was unable to walk down the aisle or stand long, I had prepared to have a wheelchair ready for her. Being the superhuman person she was she was not having that. Her determination would carry her through.

The week leading up to the wedding was great. She had strength and energy and her signature smile was back. We planned to get to Las Vegas a few days earlier than most people.

We got to Las Vegas on Wednesday which was two days before the festivities were supposed to begin. The plan was for us to enjoy a little bit of time in Las Vegas before everyone got there. When we arrived, we went to the hotel to check-in. I gave her no information about the hotel we were staying in. This was a bold move on my part because Tara had a very particular taste and wanted things to be perfect all the time. When we walked into the room, she immediately loved it. My risk in picking a room and not showing her paid off. I was able to have a few minutes of joy without worrying or planning what was next. That felt good. Unfortunately, due to the flight and all the moving around she was not able to hang out in Las Vegas as we would have liked. Her body couldn't handle it. We chose to enjoy our great room instead. I would just go get everything we needed and bring it to the room. I had no problem with that. It was like home but in a cool city in a nice hotel room with a great view. I had learned to accept and enjoy the little things. We found a way to enjoy Las Vegas even if it was from our hotel room. The Las Vega Strip view didn't hurt either.

Once our guests started arriving on Thursday night and Friday, our wedding guest started visiting us in the room. Our room quickly turned into the party room. We had as many as 15 people in the room drinking and partying together. We decided that the bachelorette/bachelor parties would take place in the room since she was going to be unable to go out. We had a good time with our friends and family. After a while, the guys left for the casino and let the ladies have their own time.

Cody Elion, Anthony Wells and I were at the casino drinking, gambling and socializing while the ladies were having a great bonding time. No one knew what would be the last time they were all together. Looking back, I am so glad that she had that time with all her friends at one time. She was surrounded by all her closest friends and relatives. It warms my heart to know she was able to have that time. When we got back to the hotel, the fellas all went our separate ways. I got back to the room to find about 6 or 7 women passed out and Tara sitting in bed watching one of our favorite television shows, Lauren Lake's Paternity Court. We had some odd TV show choices, but they were "ours".

Everything on the trip wasn't smiles and laughs. Unfortunately, we had some issues we had to work through to make the wedding day the happy day we dreamed of. All week long Tara had been telling me that her dad wasn't going to show up. I thought she was being dramatic. I had spoken to him and he was set up to drive with his brother. I stayed optimistic that he would make sure he was there to see his little girl finally get married. On Wednesday while we were on the plane waiting to take off she got a call from her dad. Just as she thought he called to inform her that he would not make it. He stated that his ride wasn't going to be able to go anymore. The timing seemed odd but that wasn't my focus. It hurt me as much as it hurt her because I know how much she loved her dad and wanted him to be there. We changed the entire destination for him to be able to attend. It would have meant everything for him to be there. He was supposed to walk his little girl down the aisle. Even though she already knew he would come she was hurt, though she didn't show it. To try and fix things I decided that if it was the ride from Colorado to Las Vegas, I would fly to Colorado rent a car and drive him myself. She wouldn't let me do it because she wanted me with her and that plan would have me in Las Vegas for the wedding ceremony only. I was ready to do anything to make her happy, but she said having me there made her the happiest. It was discouraging to not be able to fix it but her wishes came first and she wanted me with her.

Saturday, February 13, 2016, was our wedding day. Even without her dad being in attendance we planned for today to be the best day of our lives. The day started just fine until she received a call from her brother, who was supposed to walk her down the aisle in her dad's absence. He was not going to make it to the wedding either. He decided to fly standby and couldn't get on the flight even though her father was willing to pay for the tickets. This was not a surprise to Tara. She had gotten used to family members letting her down in big situations. This one hurt also because her brother was her last hope for having an immediate relative in attendance. The only family she had in town was two of her cousins. Everyone else from her side was her friends who became family. I was filled with anger after receiving that news. Why couldn't her family see what I see in her? How could you not want to be a part of such a big moment in her life? A fire was lit in me that day to never let her down like that. I would be the family she always wanted and needed.

Although I have a good relationship with my family, we are not the most tight-knit family around. We were going to be each other's family going forward.

Cody and I were out running errands to pick up the last few things we needed for the big day when I received a call from Tara informing me that her brother wasn't coming. When I hung up the phone with anger on my face Cody asked what happened. I told him what happened, and he then made a similar face like mine. After a few moments, he looked at me and said, "Screw that! I'll walk her down the aisle my damn self". Cody is just that kind of person. My best man was willing to pull double duty. That is just the kind of person he is. The only thing he cared about was helping her get down the aisle. Cody wasn't the only person who volunteered to walk her down the aisle. My dad volunteered when I called him and told him. She declined and said that both of her cousins would walk her down the aisle. That was very unconventional, and I loved the idea. Everything about it was unconventional but that's exactly what we were.

While driving around Las Vegas to get Tara the exact kind of champagne she wanted, we ended up way on the other side of town and decided we needed to stop for lunch. I got some chicken from Popeye's. Cody, on the other hand, was on a strict vegan diet. To my chagrin, we had to find a very specific type of place for him to eat. That took us to the other side of Las Vegas. While waiting for Cody to get his food, I noticed a very familiar face walking down the street. It looked like Tara's cousin Kevin Henderson. I tried to pull the car forward to see if it was him for sure, but I couldn't. I called his phone and watched him answer it. It was the most randomly beautiful moment of the day so far. He told me that he and his girlfriend were getting lunch before getting ready for the wedding. I immediately told him to call Tara. I then turned and call her myself and told her he was in Las Vegas. We got Cody's food and headed back to the hotel to rest before the ceremony. When we got to the room the makeup artist had already arrived and was working on Tara's makeup. She was in a far better mood because she had a male family member that was going to walk her down the aisle. Cousin Kevin had saved the day.

With the drama of who was coming and who wasn't behind us, we could focus on the best day of our lives. We did things unconventionally from the start. We did things unconventionally from the start. We were already legally married and we had our bachelor and bachelorette parties together-and at that moment, I was sitting in the room the entire time she was getting ready for our big day. The only thing that was traditional was her not letting me see her in her dress before the wedding. We were asked to leave so that she could finish getting dressed. So, Cody and I called for an Uber and headed to the wedding chapel. Feeling good and looking good, we took the short ride to the wedding chapel in the Westgate Las Vegas hotel. We were placed in a side room to hang out until Tara and her bridesmaids got there.

When we walked in, the moment became so real that I got nervous. While sitting in the waiting room I got a text from her cousin telling me they were running behind because she had gotten some hot flashes and even had to throw up. That call reminded me that no matter how great a day could be, she was still dealing with her illness internally. About 15 minutes later the wedding director came and brought us into the wedding chapel. Waiting there for the music to start was a moment I will never forget. Even though we were already married and had a three-person ceremony a few months before, but this made it all real. My nervousness manifested in the form of jokes. Cody and I stood upon the stage cracking jokes. The music suddenly interrupted our laughing. Our wedding had officially begun. We turned around in time to see her bridesmaid Rita turn the corner to walk down the aisle. Everyone stood up, and then it happened.

Tara turned the corner with Kevin on her arm looking so beautiful. I couldn't help but verbally say WOW! She was so beautiful during her walk down the aisle. I had to hold back my tears. I was about to marry my best friend. She was like an angel in a beautiful white dress floating down the aisle. She was walking a little slower than you would typically see, but she was holding her own. When Kevin gave her to me I expected to have to hold her up or even do the ceremony sitting in the bench they had set up just in case, she couldn't stand. True to her heart and soul, she needed no help through the ceremony. She stood strong and spoke even stronger. This was the moment we had waited for and fought for. It wasn't a huge elegant wedding, but it was exactly what we wanted. The ceremony went great. As part of the ending, we both spoke to the friends and family we had. She had the entire room crying when she described how much having everyone there meant to us. When it was my turn, I could barely get my words out. I was standing in front of everyone who had been a part of helping us get to this moment. These were people who would stay in the hospital with her when I had to go to work or run errands. These were the people who would bring food to our house or hospital to make our days easier. And lastly, these were the people who prayed for us and with us to help keep our faith strong in the face of many hardships.

Chapter 6

The Fight

After our amazing wedding weekend, we returned home to pick up where we left off. Unfortunately, the feeling of elation did not last long. Things in our lives took another turn for the worst. On March 18, just a month after our wedding, I received a call at work from my mom. She was calling to inform me that my grandmother had passed away. She told me that my cousin came home from school to check on her and found her already deceased in her bedroom. Apparently she died in the middle of praying. This came completely out of nowhere. She wasn't sick or having any issues. It was simply her time to go. This was difficult because my grandmother was one of my best friends. Tara and I had just had a conversation with her over the phone about my wedding. She had just recently received the DVD from the wedding and couldn't wait to watch it. Losing her in the blink of an eye hurt a lot. Being the angel that Tara was, she was unbelievably accommodating during this time. Out of nowhere, I had to get on a flight and fly to New York for my grandmother's funeral. This was not a trip I wanted to take for a few reasons. Losing my grandmother was, of course, one reason I didn't want to take this trip. The other reason was that it would mean I had to leave Tara home. She was unable to travel this time due to her weakened state.

Typically, I love being around my family in New York, but this trip was different. All I could think about was Tara being home alone. These thoughts bugged me so much that I changed my flight to come home 2 days earlier than originally planned. There was no way I could stay gone for three and a half days. Instead, I was only gone for a day and a half. I didn't tell her about my plans to come home early. I was able to get a flight that got me back to Atlanta before 8 am. This gave me a chance to surprise her. When I pulled up to the house I parked on the street and used the front door to keep her from hearing the garage door. When I came in I ran upstairs to find her with a look of excitement, fear, and sadness on her face. My little surprise didn't go over quite as well as I thought. She was initially scared by the door opening and someone coming up the stairs. Excitement was her next expression. It feels good to visually see someone excited by your presence. Her last reaction was sadness. I couldn't understand the sadness but then she explained that she planned to get dressed up, cook, and surprise me with a home-cooked meal. My surprise ruined her plans, and it hit her when I hopped into bed and gave her a hug. I let her know that it didn't matter. All I wanted was to be next to her. She was still a little bit sad but was more happy to have me home. These reactions meant so much because she had begun feeling ill during this time as well. Her body began to weaken again not long after returning home. Walking became very difficult.

It happened so fast that for the first time she came to me and said she wanted to go to the hospital. This was a far cry from how she was before. She would not go to the hospital unless she absolutely had to. We went to the hospital and were there for a few days. The doctors found nothing different and just changed some of her medication. Unfortunately, that didn't work. There was no change in how she felt.

What helped was when her father drove from Colorado with his two brothers to come visit us two days after leaving the hospital. They spent two-and-a-half days in town. It wasn't very long but was much needed. Like we saw in her previous trips to Colorado, being around family always made her feel better. The day that Mr. Turnbough arrived, the five of us hung out talking and having a good time. No one would know she was sick if they were just observing us. When it was time for them to head back to the hotel, Mr. Turnbough stood up and told Tara to give him a hug. She didn't feel like she was strong enough to stand and give him a hug. Instead, he came around the back of the sofa and gave her a hug from behind and a kiss on her head. I walked the three brothers outside to their car. While outside, they asked me how she was really doing. I explain to them that we have had some setbacks, but we had a plan to help build up her strength more. They left feeling good about our plans to rehabilitate her as much as we could.

When I came back to the house, she was on the couch crying. She had that baby face look she would use to get things she wanted from time to time. I saw the same look many times, but this one had tears with it. She knew I hated to see her cry for any reason, so she tried to cover them up. I quickly took my place next to her on the couch. I gave her a big hug and asked what was wrong. Her next words broke my heart. She looked at me and said, "I love my daddy so much, and he finally drove all this way just to see me, and I can't even stand to give him a hug". That moment crushed me. This one of the moments I wasn't able to be strong for her. I could feel the hurt in her body as I held her. The hurt and tears quickly transferred to me. That hurt to hear because she was a big old daddy's girl, and she waited a very long time to have that daddy's girl moment. Not being able to stand up and throw her arms around her father was devastating. As I typically did, I put on my therapist's cap and started talking to her about all the things she was able to do. I went down the list of all the times she stood up to go to the bathroom, got something from the kitchen and even answered the door. All those activities are more physically taxing than the hug she desperately wanted to give her dad. I told her that we were going to work on her building up the strength she needed to give her dad a big hug when she saw him again.

We received a call from her dad the next day, letting us know that someone else in their family had passed away in Mississippi. The brothers delayed their trip back to Colorado in order to be with their family. They would now be leaving the next day. I took the next day off from work to spend the day with Tara and make sure I facilitated her hug with her father. Two hours before they were supposed to hit the road, I went and picked him up from his hotel and brought him to the house. The three of us sat there for an hour and a half talking about our plans and what we planned to do going forward. When it was time to take him back to the hotel, he came around the back of the couch and leaned over to kiss her on her forehead again. She just reached around and put her arm behind his head. I knew at that moment that they needed that hug. I stood up and stretched my hand down to her. With a look of fear and apprehension, she grabbed it and I helped her to her feet. I then turned to him and told him she was ready for that hug.

He smiled and walked around the front of the couch, and they shared a beautiful hug. I couldn't hold back the tears. When I heard her voice say, "I love you so much daddy", I almost lost it. I loved this woman so much that a simple moment like this was unforgettable. At that moment, everything from their past didn't matter. Their time apart and at odds no longer mattered. She had forgiven all the past issues they had, and it was just daddy-daughter time. Mr. Turnbough wasn't an emotional man by any means. I could see the tears of love in his eyes as we walked to the car. On the ride to the hotel, he told me that he loved me and was proud to have me as a son-in-law. He was happy his daughter found someone with so much love in his heart for her. Before getting out of the car he again told me he loved me and that no matter what happened in the future I will always be his son. Those words struck me so hard that I again cried in the car. This hard man who never showed any emotion was sincerely accepting me. Even more impactful than that, he was confidently leaving his baby girl with me to take care of. That moment was not lost on me. I desperately wanted him to accept me as his son-in-law and family, and he did. When I got home, Tara immediately asked me to sit with her. She turned and gave me a hug and a kiss and told me she wanted to make sure I knew that she loved me and appreciated everything I had done for her. When everyone else was gone I was always there, and that gave her a peace she had never had before. My heart melted because I knew everything she had been through in the past.

We spent another couple of weeks at home trying to build her strength back up with not much success. After a few weeks, she said that she was tired of going in and out of the hospital and thought she should be admitted until they could find out what the problem was. We did exactly that. While we were there, we found out that she had fluid building up in her lungs. To remedy this, she would need a procedure to drain it. We were not very excited about it, but we agreed. She had the fluid drained and began feeling better. The doctors said they could send us home and hope that it doesn't come back; she would just need to come back once a month to see if it had built up again. The other option was to stay and be observed in the hospital. We decided to stay.

A couple of days later, the doctors noticed more fluid in the other lung. This was disturbing and meant she would need another procedure. After talking long and hard about it we decided we would do anything we needed to do to help her get better. This was a far cry from how she felt about all these procedures before. We agreed to have a procedure done to put a catheter on each side of her body so that we could drain the fluid whenever needed. This was a difficult decision because now our lives would change even more than it had before. We would have to continually check and drain each catheter. This was a process, but we were willing to undergo because we just wanted a healthy Tara. After a few more weeks, the doctors said she could go home. They would teach us how to drain and keep the catheters clean.

The doctors suggested that we a "Family Meeting". This is when all her doctors and the family sit down and come up with a plan of action. We scheduled the family meeting two days later. On the day of the meeting, there were multiple doctors in attendance. Her oncologist, palliative care doctors, and even her psychologist were in the room. As for the family, there was me, her niece, nephew, sister-in-law, and a close friend. We even had her childhood friend Renay on the phone from Colorado. During this meeting, the doctors went over everything that had happened and presented options going forward. The option that they believed in the most was admitting her into their hospice program. That was the first time I rejected something from the doctors. The only thing I knew about hospice was that it was where people go to be comfortable before they die. I was not on board with that at all. We opted to go with one of the other options and that was to have an in-home nurse come to help throughout the week so that I could go to work.

We believed that would be the best option. The doctors said ok and gave her a discharge date a couple of days away.

For the next few days, we went back to our regular routine. I would go to work in the morning and her friend Cherrelle would stay with her during the day. This had been the routine we used since the first long stint in the hospital. Cherrelle was an angel for allowing me to go to work and staying all day so Tara would not be by herself. This was amazing on both sides. Tara never had to be alone, and I was able to still work and pay the bills. One day while I was at work during one of her psychologist's visits they discussed the positives of the in-home hospice option that was presented during the family meeting. Tara made the decision to go with that once she was discharged. When I got off of work and got back to the hospital, she explained it to me and told me she made the decision. She explained that it would help in many areas. Reluctantly I got on board. There would be a real medical nurse at the house every day, another nurse would come and clean the house and tend to any of her needs, and they would provide us with everything we needed to care for her at home. They would even send oxygen tanks for her to continue using the pure oxygen to help her breathe when her lungs had fluid in them. On top of that, we stayed in a 3-level townhouse; and it would be dangerous for her to stay on the top floor and move around. They helped us rearrange the main level to accommodate her there rather than have to journey up and downstairs in her physical state. Eliminating the need to go upstairs was critical for her in her condition. They even suggested having a hospital bed brought into the house for her to lay on for comfort. That was an emphatic no from Tara. Though I understood their reasoning, I was with her. Something about that didn't feel right. We were in agreement on choosing the lesser of evils, having people at home daily and arranging the main level were not my favorite ideas, but it provided us with the support we needed at home. We were able to get behind that.

They discharged her from the hospital on Saturday, May 14, 2016. I remember it like it was yesterday. We took the scenic route home so we could see the big beautiful homes on the way. We played music and sang, laughed like we always would. The hospice administrator scheduled to meet us at the house to assess everything that was needed for the in-home care. This process moved quickly. By the end of that day, we had all the equipment and the prescriptions we needed. One of our daily nurses had come and met with us. It felt like we had our own medical team and we no longer had to worry about any issues at home because there was always a nurse on standby. The next day was a beautiful Sunday. That morning my parents had stopped by to bring a week's worth of food and drinks for her to have since they would be on a vacation that week. The sun was out, and the day seemed perfect. It was too perfect to sit in the house all day, so she asked if we could go out and enjoy the day. This process wasn't easy because she could barely walk but that never stopped us before. We went through the process of getting her outside and into the wheelchair. I rolled her around the block since our garage was on the backside of the house and she couldn't walk down the stairs to the car. Once I got her in the car, we went out for a drive. She had received some brand-new Prada shades she was excited to wear and a new braided wig. She looked amazing with her smile and radiant confidence. We spent a couple of hours out until she started getting tired. When we got home, I had to roll her around the block to the front door. By this time, she had gotten really tired so it was difficult getting her out of the wheelchair. We choose to just sit outside and play music on her phone instead. She played all the old school jams we used to love. From Ghost town DJ's "My Boo" to Nirvana's "Smells Like Teen Spirit", we were outside having a great time. From the day we met until that moment we used to always say that it didn't matter where we were, we could always have a good time. This was a prime example of that. We had a blast. Once she was able to get up and get into the house we went in to take a nap. Tara had just reconnected with our neighbor Dawn. She came over that evening and by the time she left she had volunteered to come to the house every morning after I would leave for work and stay until the nurse got there. This was amazing for my peace of mind because I never wanted her to be alone. Her being alone was my worst nightmare.

On Monday morning, I went to work early like normal. Dawn came over and stayed for a few hours, and then the nurse came. After the nurse left Dawn came back and stayed until I got home. We spent a regular night at home. We watched our normal Monday lineup of shows starting with Lauren Lake's Paternity Court. That was our last normal day.

Chapter 7

The Loss

Tuesday was a different day. I woke up around 4:30 am like I typically would. We could no longer sleep in the bed, so we slept on the couch. I got up and got ready for work first, then I got Tara's food and drinks for the day together. This morning differed from most mornings. Even though she wasn't a morning person, she would always wake up when I was up for a few minutes. This morning something was wrong. She could barely communicate with me; her breathing was off, and she seemed very weak. I refused to leave until she seemed ok. She then mustered up the strength to tell me it was ok and that the neighbor Dawn would be over shortly. Reluctantly I listened, and I headed to work. I talked to her on the phone most of the day to ease my mind about how she was. She told me it was just a rough morning and that once the nurse got there and drained the fluid from her lungs, everything was better. The nurse typically would leave around 3 pm, and then Dawn would come back. I left work a little earlier this afternoon. When I got home, we got a call from her doctor telling us that the rest of her medication was ready to be picked up. I went to pick it up and came back and cooked dinner that evening.

While cooking dinner, I noticed that her breathing was different. Her breaths seemed very shallow, and she had to work hard to get good breaths in and out. I tried to get her to tell me what she was feeling but she couldn't explain it to me. I called the night nurse to ask for some advice. She recommended that she take one pill that was prescribed to her. We had already taken that and there was no change. She then said that morphine would help. Unfortunately, morphine was one medicine that had not come in yet. I monitored her breathing, which seemed to get worse. At one point she even asked me what she should do? I spoke to the nurse again, and she said the only thing she could do was come check her out. I was able to describe the situation clearly and she said she would come if needed. After a while, her breathing went back to normal, and we went to sleep. She went to sleep; I didn't sleep much. The way she acted that night was way outside of the norm. She had gotten used to the oxygen tanks, so I knew she was getting the air she needed. It was extremely scary, so I didn't sleep. I just monitored her most of the night.

I woke up Wednesday morning, and she was in worse shape than the day before. So yet again I refused to leave until I was sure she was ok. We went through the same routine we did the morning before. I already knew Dawn would be there soon and the nurse as well. The difference this morning was that she couldn't talk to me all morning like she did the day before. I reluctantly took the hour ride to work. Around 10:00 am, I received a call from the nurse. This was a call I will never forget. The nurse asked that I come home right away. She said she did not like the shape she found Tara in when she got there. She said not to go back to work and I need to be with her all the time. I asked no questions at that point. I got up from my desk and told my manager I had to leave right now. My manager understood and let me go. On the way home, the nurse called again. To her surprise, I was already on halfway home. She then told me she needed to warn me what I was walking into. She told me that Tara had gone to the bathroom on herself and was barely conscious. She believed that she may be close to the end. I refused to believe that because I was married to a superhero. I sped home trying my best not to go crazy. When I got home, I was met at the door by the nurse. I went through my normal routine and kissed her head, both cheeks, and lips, and finished with a hug. She was very much out of it, but she always smiled when I walked into the room or spoke to her. The nurse then pulled me in the kitchen to give me the rundown. She explained that Tara had gone to the bathroom on herself and her energy was as low as it possibly could be. She even stated that Tara didn't always know who she was or what she was doing. She explained to me that some of these were the signs of everything coming to an end. She told me not to go back to work and a caseworker would complete my FMLA paperwork to secure my job while I cared for her. She then left and gave me her cell to call in case of an emergency. She left, and I took my place on the couch.

Tara spent most of the day in and out of sleep. It was far worse than any other day since we had been together. Tara woke up around 4:30 pm and amazingly snapped out of whatever it was that had her in that semiconscious state. She was energetic vibrant as she had once been. She got hungry, which she never was anymore. She asked me if I could go pick up some food for dinner. She wanted chicken and a sports drink. I ordered wings from Taco Mac and brought a few drinks home. We spent most of the afternoon watching TV and clowning around like we always would. Around 7:00 pm while we were relaxing, she suddenly burst out into a prayer of thanks. She cried out, "Thank you, Lord, thank you for everything, thank you for delivering me, thank you, thank you". I joined her in this prayer. It took me by surprise because in the mists of a terrible time in her life she was able to thank God for all he had done for us. After that, I couldn't do anything but gently hug her. She was still in pain, of course. I was just about to get up when she turned to me, grabbed my hand, looked me in the eyes and said, "Keep Going". I looked at her wondering why she would say that and replied, "Yeah WE will keep going." She just looked at me and with a small smirk said, "Ok, but you keep going". I then more forcefully reiterated that WE would keep going. She just smiled at me. Something about that interaction didn't sit well with me. Why did she come out of nowhere with that? Those words stayed in the back of my mind the rest of the afternoon.

Later in the afternoon started getting tired and wanted to take a nap. She asked me to wake her up when one of the TV shows we watch, Empire was coming on. We took a little nap together, and I woke her up at 9:00 pm as she asked. We sat and watched *Empire* that night and laughed at its ridiculousness like we usually would. Once *Empire* ended, we drained her catheter, and she tried to relax. She was having a difficult time relaxing. She could not get comfortable enough to relax and go to sleep. Typically, she would take a sleeping pill, or even take a couple of hits of some weed like a few of our nurses had suggested. As time went by, she started to breathe very erratically. It was very similar to her irregular breathing the night before. Even though she had an oxygen machine, she seemed to be gasping for air even though she would say she was breathing ok and that her breaths were just short and a little erratic. She spent the next couple of hours trying to get comfortable. A long time ago I had adopted a routine that had me staying awake every night until she was comfortable enough to go to sleep. Once she was comfortable, I would get comfortable and go to sleep myself. It took her until around 1:30 am to finally get comfortable. Since it took so long to get comfortable, I chose to just sleep sitting up so I wouldn't disturb her sleep. I leaned over, kissed her cheek and went off to sleep.

I woke up at 3:47 am like I would normally do. It was regular to wake up a few times a night and check on her. I leaned over and called her name to see if she was awake but there was no answer. When my eyes adjusted to the dark, something seemed a little be wrong. I called out her name again and there was no response. She would typically wake up since she slept so lightly. I poked her a little and her skin felt cooler than usual. I poked her harder and called out her name. She was still unresponsive.

I immediately panicked and started yelling her name while checking her breathing. She wasn't breathing, and I began having trouble breathing because of the level of panic and anxiety I was feeling. Her bones were brittle and hurt because of the cancer, so I knew I couldn't shake her too hard. In a panic, I called 911. I explained to the operator that she wasn't responding or breathing. The operator told me to put her on the floor and start CPR. I tried to softly pick her up to not hurt her, but the operator told me I needed to forget her pain and get her down. I yanked her up off the couch and laid her on the ground and began rescue breathing. The breaths didn't feel like they were going in, so they had me go straight to CPR. I was terrified for a few reasons, the first was I knew that breaking her ribs during CPR was possible and could hurt her even more, and second, the women who I loved and had given my life to was now lying lifeless on our living room floor. I frantically administered CPR for a few minutes before the EMTs came and took over. They immediately ushered me out of the house and had me sit outside. An officer sat outside with me calling family members while I hyperventilated in my chair in complete fear. I had never felt a love like this and never felt the need to give so much of myself to one person. The greatest time in my life had turned into a nightmare. The officer was able to get a hold of my friend Cody, my sister Melanie, and my grandfather John Vazquez. Cody made it to the house rather quickly and got there while I was still on the front porch. He did his best to console me but there is no way to console me at that moment. A few moments later the medic came out and regretfully informed me that their rescue attempts had failed and she was pronounced dead at 4:20 am May 19th, 2016.

All I could do was collapse into my chair and meltdown. After some time the gentleman from the coroner's office asked if I would like to go back in the house and spend a few moments with her before they took her. I agreed. By this time my grandfather had shown up. I walked over to her and laid down on the floor next to her like I typically would. All I could do was kiss her cheeks and forehead as I would usually do. I couldn't let go of her. I don't know how long I was there. I believe I zoned out for a while. Next thing I knew my grandfather was grabbing me. He told me they had to go, and I had to let them take her. Cody and my grandfather both helped me up off the ground. And held me up since I was completely weak. We were then escorted outside again while they prepared to take her. While we sat outside, my sister then arrived. I was unaware but the coroner that came was sent specifically for a veteran. After a few minutes, he came out and asked if I would like to view the flag ceremony. I agreed, and they brought us into the house. She had been placed on a stretcher and covered in a quilt-like cover. Two gentlemen in military fatigue pants came in and began the ceremony. I was unaware that this was a tradition. They brought an American flag in the house. They then stood at attention and saluted her. They then unfolded the flag one-fold at a time. She was then covered neatly with the flag. They saluted again and then they took her away. This next memory is burned in my mind forever. They rolled the stretcher out of the house and down the path towards an SUV with military sign-age on the sides. My grandfather who is also a veteran followed them to the SUV. From the patio, I could see them loading the stretcher into the truck while my grandfather stood and saluted her the entire time. I will never forget that picture for as long as I live. My grandfather tearfully saluting his granddaughter in law in a way only a military veteran could do.

I stood there for a few moments stunned and broken. Cody came and just hugged me and cried with me. They brought me into the house and laid me on the couch. I curled up and cried myself to sleep. I was awakened a few minutes later when Cody told me he had to go. I had woken him up in the middle of the night and he spent several hours with me. It was only right he continued with his morning. My sister and grandfather sat on the couch and let me be.

I woke up around 7:30 am. Upon waking up, I broke down again. I had fallen asleep in the exact same spot where she had last laid. I got myself together and called a few of Tara's relatives and gave them the news. Notifying people of someone's passing is a terribly hard thing to do, even harder when it is the person you love the most. Having to do it multiple times was like breaking into a thousand pieces repeatedly. Hearing the disbelief and pain on the other end of the phone broke me down even further. After a few more minutes my grandfather left, and it was just my sister and myself. She didn't want to leave me alone. I texted Julius, my high school friend, who happened to live in the same neighborhood. Since he has kids to take to school, I knew he would be up. I texted him and told him what happened, and he came right over. When he got there, my sister left. He was exactly who I needed at that time. I needed someone who would let me go through all the emotions that someone could have during this time. He talked when I needed to talk, and he just sat there silent when I needed to be silent. The important thing was he would not leave me alone. We spent a few hours just sitting there. After a while, he said we need to get out of the house and get some fresh air. He took me to a park around the corner I never knew existed. There was a walking trail through the woods. We walked, talked. In that terribly dark time it was a quick escape. I will always thank Julius for that. It was more helpful than he knew.

After that, I went back home and went to sleep. When I woke up all I could do was lay on the couch doing nothing. I couldn't eat or watch T.V. I could only turn on the gospel music station Tara used to listen to all the time. I just laid there for hours. I received a text message from one of my best friends, Ricky Whitley. His text read, "Where are you right now?". I responded and told him I was at home. He told me he was on his way home and told me to pack a bag and come to his place. He said he wasn't going to let me stay by myself tonight. He had spoken with his fiancé and she had made up a room for me. After a couple of hours, I got dressed and went over there. Ricky and I sat on the balcony just talking most of the night. The next morning, I woke up and headed home to try to put things back together. As I was driving home, all I could do was cry. I was crying for a lot of reasons. My wife was gone, I was lonely, was in disbelief and scared of the future without my one true love. It is an impossible feeling to shake. I just wanted to be alone. I got home and cleaned up the house. Then I took a nap. I was awakened from a call from Julius. He told me he was on his way home and had bumped into an old classmate of ours and mentioned me. He asked if it was ok if he brought our classmate with him. I was fine with that. So, they came over and we hung out for a few hours. Once they left I crashed on the couch. I was tired of being around people. I knew that people said not to be alone, but I handle things differently. I needed time alone.

When I woke up Sunday morning, I began planning her home-going ceremony. My grandfather got me in touch with the funeral home that was used for my grandmother's funeral. The funeral director contacted the veteran's administration to get everything taken care of. I began contacting family and friends to advise them that the funeral would be on May 26th at my parent's church. As the planning was going on, there was a situation I was not ready to tackle. That situation was if I should stand up and speak at the funeral. I really don't like public speaking and in the mental state I was in, I didn't believe I could do. The issue came from the fact that I knew for a fact that no one knew her the way I did. There are people who knew her for her entire life and I just knew her for the past few years. The thing is, I knew her how everyone else knew her, but I also knew the person she had become over the last three or four years. I knew that I needed to speak for her, but I didn't feel like

I could. I held off until the very last minute when we needed to have the programs completed and printed. I decided it meant more to tell our story than to be too scared and let a golden moment pass by.

The night before the ceremony, I wrote a few notes that I wanted to talk about. I was led to speak about love and always having fun. Tara was the funniest person I have ever met. She made me understand that I was acting old and not fully living by not having as much fun as possible. The second thing I was led to speak about was love. We both thought we knew what love was before we met. We thought we had just been unlucky until we met. We quickly found out there was more to love than we ever thought, and we worked every day to continue to build and grow closer. Through that, we forged a bond that could never be broken. We had what most people call true and forever love. And the last thing I wanted to speak about was the ability to *keep going*. Like I stated before, she stressed to me in her last conversation to *keep going*. That wasn't just a message for me. That was a message for everyone. No matter what you're going through, you must *keep going*. I believe that she is continuing to *keep going*, just not in physical form.

When I woke up on May 26th, 2016, I moved throughout the house, streets, and stores and into the church like I was still in a Spike Lee movie. It was like I was standing still, and the world was moving around me. I couldn't put my emotions into words that day. The ceremony started, and I sat in the front row listening to the poems, prayers and the people who spoke before me. When it was my turn, I asked Tara for strength and took my place at the podium. I asked my friends to join me on stage for support. I stood there with my closest friends behind me and spoke from the heart. I followed my notes but just as a guide to keep me on schedule. I only had to pause three times for the tears, which given what I felt that day was a great job. I finished by telling my beautiful wife Tara, "I Love You Always," and then took my seat. Kendall Ficklin delivered a great message and then they played a slide show that my mother created. It was a slideshow of pictures from her whole life. It was set to a song called "There Will Be a Day". The song says that there will come a day when there will be no more tears, a day when we will all be together again in heaven. I can't hear that song without crying anymore. The service went off well and then we headed to the cemetery.

At the cemetery, the Air Force sent a group out to play Taps and a group for the flag presentation. The same flag that they draped over her the night she passed was then folded and presented to me on behalf of the President of the United States. Even though I know he didn't send them to the funeral or sign the certificate they gave me, it still made me feel good to think these things were presented to me in her honor by President Barack Obama. Tara was a big Obama supporter and really loved everything he was about as a man. So that moment felt good. The good feeling was short-lived because shortly after that, they had me carry the urn with her ashes to the columbarium she would be placed in. I carried the urn and placed inside the columbarium and they closed it up. Just like that, it was all over. Everyone went home, and I went home with a few friends. Once they left, I was back home all by myself. This is when it all hit me. I was now alone in the world again. Not that my family and friends are not here for me, but it was different. I was told once that the family you choose ends up being more connected than the family you don't. That may sound crazy to some, but I believe it to be true. I know that I will never love anyone the way I love Tara Morris. I stayed home for the next couple of weeks.

I decided that I couldn't just stay in the house and wither away, so I booked a room up at Lake Oconee for Memorial Day. I asked my brother from another mother Jabari to go with me and he did with no questions. We went up there with no plans. I just needed to get away. We went up there and had lunch and dinner at a restaurant right on the lake. We went fishing, sightseeing, and even shopping at the local Goodwill. That was one of Tara's favorite pastimes. It was a good couple of days for my soul which I felt had been ripped out of my body.

Chapter 8

The Mission

Upon returning from the lake, I had a decision to make. I needed to decide if I was going to keep going or just give up. Well, there wasn't much to think about because I knew that Tara would never condone me just giving up. She would come back and haunt me forever if I did. She told me to *Keep Going* so that is what I had to do. So how do you keep going when your entire world has collapsed? How do you pick up the pieces? Well, that is a process. I choose to start with two things I know Tara wanted badly for me. The first was to get my degree. She had offered to pay for it a few weeks before her passing. The second was to create the foundation we had talked about for a while. It was to focus on helping young athletes pursue their dreams and to support young women in making the right decisions in their young lives. I had a conversation with my friend Brandon about the foundation. In a moment of pure genius, he said I should call it the *Keep Going Foundation* since she stressed to me to keep going. I almost fell out of my seat when he told me that. With tears in my eyes, I decided that the *Keep Going Foundation* would be the mission I was on to further her legacy. Tara was my reason for waking up every day. Losing her was earth-shattering and something I will never get over. I continue to use it to further the legacy of a great woman who did not have the chance to show the world how much of a force she could be for good. I believe that will also be what helps me heal my broken heart.

The search for peace of mind began. I went from spending every hour of the day caring for someone to complete emptiness and silence. When you're going through something, traumatic silence can be deadly. Being alone with just your thoughts can lead you down a dark path. Many times as I wanted to give up, but I couldn't let that happen. I had spent countless hours trying to keep Tara out of that dark place, so I couldn't let myself go there. The hard part is figuring out how to do that? That's a question I needed to find the answer to fast.

I received a text from a childhood friend who shared with me that he too had lost his significant other and had been dealing with it for a few years. He stressed to me to focus on the things that make me happy. He told me that I should talk to people who understand and can help feed my soul. He told me stories of how he went down the wrong path and was taken over by drugs and alcohol. He begged for me to contact him if I felt like I was going down that path. I promised I would not go that route but that I would call him if those thoughts came into my mind. That was one of the moments that taught me not to hold things in. There are people who may be able to help you even if they aren't in your life daily.

Being completely honest with myself I knew I needed help. I just wasn't sure what kind of help. I prayed every day for God to guide me on how to navigate life going forward. I chose to see a counselor at my parent's church. I signed up for counseling sessions once a week for a couple of months. I went with an open mind understanding that the only way to heal is to be completely honest. After a month I didn't feel like I was getting what I needed. I've always grown up in church and continued into adulthood. I've always known prayer, and it seemed like the only answer I got from each session was a prayer. I appreciated the time and the words from my counselor, but I needed more clinical help. After my last session at church, I began to look for a clinical counselor. One day I was at work and happened to get a glance at a picture we took on vacation. At that moment, I had a random mid-day breakdown at my desk. I quickly made it to the bathroom where I spent about fifteen minutes sobbing in a bathroom stall. When I was done I got myself together and went back to work. After the breakdown, my supervisor noticed something was wrong and told me about the employee assistance program. This program would provide me with free clinical sessions and discounted sessions to use when the free ones were used. I soon began going to weekly sessions again. This time it was a little different. My counselor took a different approach to my mental health. He created an action plan for me to accomplish the goals that Tara and I had prior to her passing. This action plan gave my life a purpose I wasn't sure I had anymore. He told me something I will never forget. He told me that nobody can dictate how I recover and that my timetable is on me and me only. He made me understand that my path was to be traveled by me alone and at the pace I need. I needed to hear that because people tried to put pressure on me to get back to normal. I was in no rush to get back to normal. I didn't even know what normal was anymore. The timing of this meeting was perfect. It was perfect because I was feeling self-conscious about my need to go to the cemetery every weekend. The counselor made me understand that my healing process was my journey. I continued to go to the cemetery every Saturday morning. I still go multiple times a month and always before my football games. I'm not sure that will ever end. Tara was the single biggest fan I've ever had, and she never let me give up on football even when she asked me to quit baseball for a while. It was important for me to always honor here throughout my football career.

The second action step we discussed in my sessions was staying busy. The counselor asked me about what I do outside of work and sports. I told him about the foundation I started. He thought it was an amazing endeavor and pushed me to continue to throw myself into it. He said that she would live through the foundation and the good works we do. I told him about her plans to work with and mentor young women. Her spirit would help to power *Keep Going Foundation Inc.* That was what I did. The mission was set, and the plans were put in motion.

I began drawing out plans for an event that would influence the community and promote activity. If we were going to make an impact, we had to show people we were a worthy cause and one that could help many people. Our very first project was an equipment drive. We would collect new and used equipment and redistribute it to young athletes in need. This was a successful project that is still running today. To date, we have provided 126 young athletes with equipment for the sports they play. We have provided baseball gloves, cleats for multiple sports, football pants, mouthpieces, gloves, and footballs. We've provided backpacks and school supplies as well. We love the feeling of handing a young person something that they need to help them keep going. We know we have given them a chance. Our second project came when a high school classmate of mine reached out to me and told me she saw what I was doing and passed my information on to a friend who could possibly need our assistance. This friend reached out to me on social media. She sent me a message telling me about her daughter that played volleyball in high school. She stated, the season didn't go quite as planned and her daughter didn't get looked at by colleges. She needed more exposure to ensure she was recruited and had a possibility at a scholarship. She went on to say that she made a club team that helps with exposure, but it was expensive. As things go, we received our very first donation the day before from a childhood classmate from back in New York. The donation was a money order for $250. We took that money and donated the $250 dollars to the young girl's fees for the team. About three weeks later, we received an email update showing that she had been accepted to the team and all her fees were paid. Some months later we received another update from the young lady's mother proudly alerting us that she had gone on a few college visits and would be accepting a scholarship to Georgia Institute of Technology to play volleyball. This was a pivotal moment in my healing. I watched a person I had never met before ash for help. It was a total stranger looking for help and the day before I received an out of nowhere donation. It was a no brainer to turn around and donate that money. More than just helping a young girl, it showed me that the plan put in place between my counselor and myself was working. It also showed me that Tara was also still in my corner and working behind the scenes to make this movement a success. The young lady we were fortunate enough to aid is now attending one of the best schools in the country and we were a part of making that happen. We were on the right path.

We needed to continue this momentum and put some more projects together. What we learned from helping the young lady was that vision for helping others is great, but it would take funds to continue to do so. We knew we wouldn't randomly receive funds just because someone needed them. We were going to have to build a fundraising campaign. With that in mind, we decided to think big. We decided we would have a huge end-of-year fundraiser. This fundraiser would be our biggest event of the year. After doing some thinking, we came up with a casino themed fundraiser. The idea came from a couple of company parties I had attended in the past. I had a great time and recalled that we didn't use real money and prizes were awarded at the end of the night. After doing some research, we found that casino themed fundraisers were not rare. So, I began the planning process for the next event.

Planning an event like this is not easy, and I had never done anything like this before. It was quite overwhelming. It was made more overwhelming given that I had committed to the event and since it is in Tara's honor, it could not fail. I hired an event planner, but it didn't work out with her. I began to work on my own. Shortly thereafter, I began communicating with a childhood friend from New York. Our communication began to increase and before long she was coming to visit. We started dating long distance. She would come visit and we would talk every day. Through our communications, I let her in on what I was doing and why. I told her my vision, and she was completely on board. She believed in what I was doing and began handling all the administrative tasks and event planning. She was the perfect person to have in my life at that time. She was an amazing person to be with, and she was also a great help with all the tasks we had. This was a huge help because she was the kind of person that loved event planning and idea creation. Moreover, she believed in me. She quickly took control of much of the planning and fundraising. During this process, we became even closer. Was this happening? I thought I had found someone that could help me keep going. We planned the event and before you could blink the event date came and it was a success. It wasn't an overwhelming success because it didn't raise as much money as planned. What it did was promote the foundation very well. Even though it didn't bring in much money, it did wonders for showing the world what we are about. Everything seemed to be getting better. I started a company to honor my wife, put on a large event and even met a girl I believe could help me heal and move on. That turned out to be the exact opposite.

Chapter 9

The Transition

Things between the new women and myself were great for months. After a while, things started to get rocky. It was a long distanced relationship, and we had some fundamental differences in our views of the world. I made some mistakes and so did she. Having a personal and business relationship complicated things further, especially when we had some issues surrounding the things that happened concerning the fundraiser. All the great feelings we had personally and professionally began to change. I don't believe either of us was completely ready for a relationship. She had been recently been divorced after being married 10 years, and I had lost my wife only two years earlier. Our communication consistently declined over time, and then everything ended abruptly on my birthday. I had gotten a terrible cold and was stuck in bed. I called her that morning and talked to her for a few minutes. The call wasn't like most. It felt like I was talking to a stranger who wasn't excited to speak to me and didn't seem to care. We spoke for about 20 minutes. The last words I heard from her for over 6 months was "I hope you feel better and I will call and check on you a little later. Get some rest" I did not hear her voice again until September when she decided to reach to me and condemn me for the mistakes I made months earlier. We had our back and forth and things finally ended.

I had a lot of anger and resentment in my heart because I believed she was a coward for how she broke up with me. She told me in the very beginning that above everything we were friends first and would always be friends even if a romantic relationship didn't work. She also said she believed in my foundation so much she would always be a part of it. All of that went out the window when she walked out of my life. It caused a lot of resentment in me. This anger only helped to fuel my downward spiral. Not long after that, I began to feel the effects of putting on such a big event without great financial backing. I quickly fell into debt. After trying many ways of coming up with more money, I was eventually evicted from my apartment. I had taken on too much debt to recover with just my day job. I had to deal with a nasty breakup, terrible financial situation while still trying to heal from the loss of my wife. This was a turning point in my healing. I had to decide how I was going to get out of this hole. I thought about going into some illegal businesses to make some fast money. That idea didn't last long because I felt that it would disrespect everything I was doing. I couldn't feel good about funding my community organization with illegal money. Up until that point, things had been going well with all my projects and each one made me feel just a little better. I felt like I was healing through all my works, and this was a major setback.

I started out staying in decent hotels but that got expensive quickly. Then I started staying in extended stay hotels, which was better but still expensive. I figured if I could hold on for a little while I could get a new apartment and start over. This proved to be more difficult than I planned. I was stressed out all the time but put on the mask of being fine every day. As of right now, nobody knows about any of those situations. After about a month of staying in different hotels, I had no choice but to stay in my car. This was one of the lowest points in my life. It never occurred to me that I had become homeless until I had to sleep in my car and shower at people's houses, different gyms, and even my job. This became a routine. To conceal this, I would sleep in my car for two or three nights a week and then I would spend another two or three nights at a friend or my parents. I told them that it was more convenient with my sports schedule to stay there. When you are homeless, you have to become very creative if you are going to hide it from the world. The last trick I would use is to hang out with some close friends and just crash on their couch. Every night I would craft a plan for the next day. The most difficult part of being homeless was figuring out how to not be homeless. I know that sounds weird and elementary, but it's true. Being homeless is expensive. There are many things that you must pay for or spend money on just to maintain. This went on for months. I used sports and activities as a cover for a lot of things when trying to hide the truth. Somehow through this time I still put on 3 of my Athlete Development Workshops and donated equipment and money to the young people my company supports. Think about that, a homeless person continuing to give to others. I was either really smart or really dumb. I don't know, but this situation showed me where my heart was. I've always believed that you receive more blessings from blessing other people. I prayed that I could get myself together to more effectively help others.

Fast forward to September when I was supposed to start the process of putting on my next Casino Royale. It quickly became clear that it was not going to happen. This marked the moment where I had to make a choice. The choice was to give up on everything and work only for me or to develop an action plan to finally get out of this hole. I chose to get out of the hole. I really had no choice. I started a company in my wife's honor and called it Keep Going Foundation. I couldn't possibly give up. I had a stronger reason to continue fighting than to give up. My "why" was stronger than my "why not". Rather than partake in illegal activities, I began finding ways to make small amounts of money. I would train athletes, come into work fifteen minutes early and leave fifteen minutes late to work on different projects to earn extra money, and even sold many personal effects. I began to train myself to not waste time on things that were not moving me forward. When your back is against the wall, your only choice is to fight your way out. I began to fight back. As frustrating as it was at times I would always tell myself, " just keep going". "Tara told you to keep going, and you made a promise. Just keep going." Through this new mindset, I was able to start bringing in extra money to put to the side. Putting money to the side when you have no place to stay and you sleep in a cold car without any heat is hard. I had to keep the bigger picture in mind. I would sit up late at night in either a hotel parking lot or in a gated apartment complex I could gain access to. I would cry and pray, pray and cry. It was the weakest I had ever been. One night, while sitting in the car I remembered the words told to me by an old friend after my wife passed. He said that you need to get your feelings out somehow. I hate writing because I'm not any good at it and I'm not musically inclined. As I sat in the car one night, the only thing I could think about was how to get my feelings out. I grabbed a pen and paper and began writing. As I wrote, more and more thoughts and feelings came to mind. I let it all bleed on the paper. Recalling memories good and bad would literally have me in tears. I had let my beautiful wife down by falling so far down. She would be ashamed of what my life had deteriorated to. Those feeling fueled me to keep writing. Her words, keep going played in my head on repeat. That drove me to keep plugging along. Before long I started believing that maybe my words could help. With no money in my bank account I reached out to a publisher that I knew of from a group I joined after my wife passed. After speaking with her, I knew I was going to have to step out on faith and make something happen. I did a lot of research on writing books. The process seemed very intimidating and very expensive. Through my research, I kept coming back to the same publisher. Something about this company felt like it was more than a publishing company. As weird as it may sound it felt like home. It felt like this company could help me heal while helping me publish a book. So, I chose this company even though I had no money. All I knew was that I couldn't fall any further. I blindly signed up even though I wasn't sure how I was going to pay for it. What I did was paint myself into a corner to ensure I had no choice but to put in the work needed to change my situation. On that day my mind shifted to not worrying about my current situation and I stepped out on faith.

Chapter 10

The Bounce Back

A huge life decision was made, so now I needed to focus on bouncing back. Everything came down to doing the work I needed to do to make it happen. My life changed for the better after that. Though I was still homeless, I didn't feel like it. It may sound crazy, but I found my purpose and nothing else mattered. I would pray for guidance and help to focus. On occasion, I would pray for a blessing. This went on for months. Then one day while at Cody's house doing my normal hangout and crash routine, he told me he saw what I was doing and believed in it. He made me an offer that would change everything. He told me he wanted to see me win and what I was doing he believed in and wanted to help. He said that he would take on a payment or two for the publisher or anything that was holding me back. I declined the offer the first time he proposed it to me. Pride wouldn't let me take money from someone else. After praying about my situation one night, it hit me. I've been praying for a blessing or some relief and it had come. My pride has never let me ask for money in any amount more than $20. That blessing came, and it came in a form I never thought about. I changed how I operated and changed my mindset. That mindset change showed someone who was able to help me that I was a good bet. I eventually took the blessing and was able to start getting things back on track. I took care of some debt that was eating up my paychecks first. Then I began having a portion of my paycheck go into a separate savings account. During this time, I got serious about adding another stream of income, so I began to seriously work on my athlete performance training. I began to earn extra money for training athletes. When I stopped focusing on my bank account and started focusing on becoming better in every aspect of my life, things started changing. Numerous wise people told me that money is the last thing to come. It cannot be the focus. That was my approach and things started to happen. I received a well-timed bonus at work around the same time I received a payment for a team I was coaching. Since I paid down the debt that was eating up my paychecks I was now in a place where I had money after paying all essential bills. Even after putting my monthly publishing payment aside I was still able to put some money to the side. One of the biggest life adjustments I made was involving God in my daily life more often. That part of my life had taken a hit over the past couple of years. I am living proof that prayer works. The results didn't come when I wanted them to. The results came when I was ready from them. As I am writing this I am getting ready to put a deposit down on a new apartment and the work I needed to be done on my car to keep it running is scheduled to be done in a couple of weeks. My current job is going well. My businesses are growing, and I am finally gaining some peace in my life. The step that means the most to me is that I am now able to return to visiting Tara's grave with peace in my heart. I had gone over six months without visiting her because I was ashamed.

Reconciling how my life had fallen apart without her was too much. She had taught me better and prepared me for the world and I had been failing her. I can return and have peace in my heart when I did. I've even started waking up each day with a smile on my face ready to tackle new adventures. I almost feel as though I've been reborn. When I was at my lowest, all I was able to do was stay faithful, positive, and work. It sounds simple but can be the opposite if your mind isn't in the right place. It's amazing how staying faithful through the tough times and shifting your mindset can better your situation. Having people who believe in you and support you in being the best person you can be is pivotal in growing through tragic loss. The most important part of bouncing back is always having a strong "why". Having a strong "why" is what will keep you focused on your goals. If you have no reason why you are doing something, you will fall short. I'll no longer fall short. Moving forward is the only option. I was sent an affirmation I look at every day, "A journey of a thousand miles starts with just one step", and I plan to keep taking one step at a time with full confidence I will reach the destination God has planned for me. Through tough times, I will always remember my "why". I kept going because my amazing wife Tara told me to. She was my why and now making her proud is my "why" So, my words to all I meet are Keep Going, Keep Growing.

Made in the USA
Monee, IL
11 June 2020